WHAT IS BROKEN BINDS US

WHAT IS BROKEN BINDS US

LORNE DANIEL

Brave & Brilliant Series
ISSN 2371-7238 (Print) ISSN 2371-7246 (Online)

© 2025 Lorne Daniel

University of Calgary Press
2500 University Drive NW
Calgary, Alberta
Canada T2N 1N4
press.ucalgary.ca

All rights reserved.

No part of this book may be reproduced in any format whatsoever without prior written permission from the publisher, except for brief excerpts quoted in scholarship or review.

This is a work of fiction. Names, characters, businesses, places, events, and incidents are either the products of the author's imagination or used in a fictitious manner. Any resemblance to actual persons, living or dead, or actual events is purely coincidental.

LIBRARY AND ARCHIVES CANADA CATALOGUING IN PUBLICATION

Title: What is broken binds us / Lorne Daniel.
Names: Daniel, Lorne, author
Series: Brave & brilliant series ; no. 44.
Description: Series statement: Brave & brilliant series, 2371-7238 ; no. 44 | Includes bibliographical references.
Identifiers: Canadiana (print) 20250203979 | Canadiana (ebook) 20250203987 | ISBN 9781773856384 (hardcover) | ISBN 9781773856391 (softcover) | ISBN 9781773856407 (PDF) | ISBN 9781773856414 (EPUB)
Subjects: LCGFT: Poetry.
Classification: LCC PS8557.A53 W43 2025 | DDC C811/.54—dc23

The University of Calgary Press acknowledges the support of the Government of Alberta through the Alberta Media Fund for our publications. We acknowledge the financial support of the Government of Canada. We acknowledge the financial support of the Canada Council for the Arts for our publishing program.

The manufacturer's authorized representative in the EU for product safety is Mare Nostrum Group B.V., Mauritskade 21D, 1091 GC Amsterdam, The Netherlands. Email: gpsr@mare-nostrum.co.uk

Editing by Helen Hajnoczky
Cover image: AdobeStock 1197685179
Cover design, page design, and typesetting by Melina Cusano

for Sandi

Contents

1
LESSONS IN EMERGENCY PREPAREDNESS | 1

Lessons in Emergency Preparedness | 3
Crushed | 7
An Opening for the Uninvited | 8
The Breaks | 10
Sing Vibratos of Light | 13
With Wonder | 14
Body Sensing Practice | 16

2
WHEN THE TRIBUTARIES RAN RICH | 19

Giving Back: the Dream | 21
My Place at the Corner | 22
What Has Taken Place | 24
My Time Little | 27
When the Tributaries Ran Rich | 28
The Plow and What Follows | 30
Tack, Harness, Lash | 32
Lang may yer lum reek | 34
Ways to Find Family in a Forest | 35
Accordion Map | 37

3
IN THE FAMILY NAME | 39

Kettling | 41
Approaching Magnolia | 44
In the Family Name | 47
Fugue and Spiritual | 50

4
EPISODIC TREMOR & SLIP | 53

Night, Vectors | 54
Fluency (First Loss) | 56
Play Bonded | 58
Episodic Tremor and Slip | 59

5
UNTIL THE SEAS GRACE YOU | 73

In the Family Support Circle | 74
Until the Seas Grace You | 75
Alarm Will Sound | 76
Conscripts | 77
Search | 78
Chasm and Divide | 79
Our Kit | 81
You Don't Get Here Without | 82

6
IN A SMALL CRAFT IN THE CURRENT | 83

In a Small Craft in the Current | 84
Emergency Triolets Breakdown | 86
What Does Not Fall | 87
Hush | 88
Lift | 89
wet/land/air | 90

7
ELDERS AND THE LIGHT | 91

Maple and Oak and the Light They Hold Aloft | 92
Witness in the Water | 93
A Run on Flowers | 95
Absence, Not False | 96
The Thing | 98
when a loved one dies | 99
To Carry an Absence | 100
Grave Work | 101
Biking to the Green Burial Grounds | 102

▽

Notes | 103
Acknowledgements | 105

Live in the space of fractures.
Make visible the loss.

—Saidiya Hartman

1
LESSONS IN EMERGENCY PREPAREDNESS

Lessons in Emergency Preparedness

1. Readiness

We could handle things, first
wife and I. Proudly
poor and adulting hard
those first 500 days out
of college—first baby
in our laps, first "permanent" job.
Benefits and bureaucracy, hand in hand.
High over Edmonton, 21st floor, my degree
unframed under magnets on the fridge. Baby food.
We learned
to keep an emergency bag by the door
for the 3 a.m. false alarms, when
some joker tripped a pull station
and we shared the joy of 21 flights down,
21 back up with the baby while fire crews
clomped about to reset alarms and elevator,
check glass panels, coiled hoses.

We could handle that. When the clock alarm
threw me out into morning's rush
I would clamber onto my rusted one-speed
with its great sweeping handlebars
—wide as albatross wings—
and wheel urgently to the Office
of Emergency Preparedness where
where my important qualification
was being decades younger
than the others—retired cops, vested
early Forces retirees, Mitch the Vietnam vet.

Every morning everyone signed in
—15 minutes early was the unwritten rule—
hung jackets on assigned hooks, disappeared
into assigned cubicles for each deadly day
of pushing paper and watching the clock

mounted over our identical government-issue desks.
Seeing me duck into place
not quite late every day, Mitch would wink.
I was young.
That bike had wings.
I could fly.

2. Inventory

You need to know that Mitch had the best wink.
Just the corner of one eye,
a wee dimple in the cheek. Everyone knew
he meant mischief.
Friday afternoons at month-end
were reserved for inventory and this was a skill
Mitch thought I needed, one not taught
where I had been schooled. It meant
claimable mileage on the preferred, indirect, route
to the East End warehouse far
from the buttoned-down office.
Nothing ever changed
at the warehouse, we Officers
all knew: the crates of taste-free meal
replacement packs, the emergency flares
best before some date when half of us
would be dead, the great bundles
of blankets. Inventory took a minute
initialling the ten-page checklist, followed
by adjournment for a couple hours
at a seedy little East End tavern
where there was no risk
of the Senior Officers walking in,
their preferences more upscale, West End.
Mitch winked. I smiled and lifted
a cheap draught.

3. Breaktime

I was impressionable but I wasn't the only one
who followed Mitch like a big brother.

The grown men, as I called them
at home, they jumped too
to follow the big guy for pickup games, hoops
at St. Vincent Catholic School
(none of us Catholic). Mitch
(also not Catholic), who could score
anything, scored the free gym time, drove
and dunked, noon hours that summer.
Our Canadian hockey skills useless
in the face of his dribbling, laughing, Yankee
swagger. Flushed and taunting.

And when Mitch slammed
the pine under the hoop
after a layup one day, slapped
down flat and hard on that broad back

there was a rush, suddenly, of nothing.

We fell silent, we
Emergency Preparedness Plan writers,
our faces blank white, our stupid
dollar store ties on the floor
by the door, socks too, barefooted
bureaucrats all. Standing around
his immense chest,

stilled. No plan. I checked my wrist
for some reason, then the wall
clock, the school gym. It was 12:25,
the second hand still, improbably,
moving.

Crushed

The bad news this week relentless, rolling
past my glazed face. Addictions,
elections, deaths of the wrong
people, hypnotic grief. Dazed
at the roadside today I inhale hot exhaust.

Blurred tires hiss, rut and groove,
the grey nothing just a step away.
Over, over.
On the shoulder, waiting for a break,
me and this sleek crow, its cape
tucked and trim. Light disappears
or plays, iridescent, depending
on the moment, the angles between us.

A semi blows by and I am struck
by that unruffled coat, the shining
absence of concern. Unblinking.
Legs spring-loaded, ready
to jump to some small grain,
fresh-crushed and nourishing.

An Opening for the Uninvited

The ocean rolls up with animal energy
this morning. Saltwater foaming
from the mouth of the world. Surfpound
on sand—flat hard and smooth. Pound,
gather back, pound in again.

You can navigate a zone here between
the insistent pulse and the speargrass, the rough
line of land's edge, uninvited
yet not quite unwelcome. The foreshore
would have you believe, this morning,
that you can roll with the rumble
and retreat, rise
and decline. Grief ebbs
like water—slipping back
down the sand. Bubbling, almost
disappearing into itself.

Carrying always the knowledge
of tectonic plates. At times and places
like this you can dig toes into sand, can imagine
your own bones knitting, fascia, tendon,
connective tissue growing
strong as scars. What the living
tissues of this world do.

>   what snaps
>   —snaps you to—
>   is low
>   motion at eye's edge
>   there   there
>   circling
>   spiraling
>   in
>   tight and close
>   closer

        the flat broad shoulders
        wide animal skull
        lowered
        —*that breed*—
        jaw set
        heading for ankles
        and you alone, weapon-less, empty-handed
        bare legged
        heart and flesh
        neckpulse
        fully merely human

and in the moment you remember not to lock eyes with a predator
someone whistles far off and just like that the animal
lopes off across sand barely leaving a print. Abandoning
you like the rollers abandon driftwood at high tide.

How quickly this becomes little, a little
emergency averted, like all those times you,
the new parent, would rise parental over a day's
flung food, big bills, broken bones, homes, windows.
When you are composed, safe
as a poem, you almost laugh
as you step into rough
edge grass, take up a stick—blackened,
sharpened, hardened in someone else's fire,

raise the charred limb
against a world that wishes you
nothing.

The Breaks

In something less than a moment, that shear
between one life and whatever this is. Next.
A sharp fragment of nothing, like a knife
that cut clean without touching
what it separated.

Just like that, like nothing, my eyes open
level with paving
stones. Red brick. Pocked red brick.
Unmoving.

I am him. He is here. Someone
else
        gone.

        should we call an ambulance?
        can you feel this? this?
        how much pain is this
        on a scale, one to ten?

He was biking, wheeling
with a certain grace, I thought,
ready for a coffee break one moment

                                                then the next.

What was the time frame? How broken
into lines angles   shards
am I?

        seconds as big
        as a breath
        that won't come
        sucker punched by who / what?
        the fall and hard
        stop   a pop
        through some fragile line
        into blank   pale   vacant   space

Lungs inadequate to release
a body of pain beyond what the bones
or brain can negotiate, in the marrow
of deep memory, what was once safely just
there.

An ambulance, a jarring ride, the bowl
of my body not holding. Sacrum.
Sacred bone. Holy bone.

Carlos the kind orderly delivers me
to Duane, surly xray tech
     S'pozed to be my day off
Close enough to read his tag, I plead
for helpers
     there's no one around
balls my gurney sheet into two
angry, makeshift handles, drags me
two-fisted from gurney to his machine

my screams heard by my wife
down the empty corridor.
     Wasn't s'pozed to be here today
You and me too.

Carlos rescues me, whispers a little
secret from the back room. *Fractura mayor.*
No shit. Holy crap.

  Dilaudid dream floating on
  through a brain somewhere
  detached paddling through the melt
  of hot pain like a summer boy
  not there

It's a jigsaw, the socket in three. I learn
to pronounce *a-ce-TAB-u-lum,* the big plate
of the pelvis, how the hard stone hammered
my own femur through. Bone through bone.

We need to put the cup back together, says Dr. Stone,
one big hand cupping a fist, spelling it out
anterior open reduction internal fixation of the acetabulum.
Reduction. Fixation. Being fixed, repaired, becoming
fixated. *We do this all the time.*
Put people back together.

*We used to lose a lot of people
like you, back in the day,* says today's day shift nurse,
just being pleasant, chitchatting with me the patient in bed 14B,
all we had was traction. Not, of course, meaning
to get a grip and get going
but the opposite: not going anywhere, a weight
tied to your foot, giving gravity some extra pull.
We used to lose people.

       minddrift   deadend
       hallways *pneumonia* *clots*
       blood jammed up in the wound
       breaks free   heads to the heart
       or brain   a final stop

Stone is saying something to me about sticky bones,
I want those sticky bones, meaning to help
me understand about a body's glue and growing back.
Casually he says the surgery was *life threatening
but you're all good now.*
A good, sutured thing.

Pinned   titanium   screwed   now nurses
here to tilt   pieces of me up shoulders first
swing   ankles over the edge   into some unknown   space

shaky as memory

Sing Vibratos of Light

He lifts and steps the rubber-footed
walker down hollow corridors, a new wing.

Vaulted ceilings sing vibratos
of light, quiet rooms offer

to cradle. Plush. Pain-free. He rests
afresh. In this his fine new state

he drifts until—a vessel rapping up
against a gentle dock—he wakes:

the whisperless hall of night. His
only worry now that he must return

to the familiar before he is missed.
Someone, surely, will be looking, will

they not? Though there are no nurses,
no orderlies here. Pull heavy legs from sweaty sheets,

swing to a grim sit, on the edge, bend
to plunge headlong back into cacophony.

With Wonder

Flat on our backs on the front room futon, the baby
coos and spits and kicks little pink-clad crab legs
and I follow her eyes to the off-white ceiling, dancing

sparkles in the plaster. I clutch a pillow
against complicated chuckle-shudders that want to run
away down my left side. Between us, the cat crouches, pettable

in that wary cat way. Radar ears at work. I wonder
if this is happiness, or
something close. I'm freshly back and proud

to be self-propelled again, fingerless
gloves on the hard rubber tires of my chair,
pumping me around the block. Part way there,

anyway. It's steeper and longer
than I remember. There are cracks
where I don't roll so smoothly. *Even so*

it's good to take a breather, I say to no one
in particular. Or myself. That tiny, tiny, white blossom
there, in the cracked mortar of the rock wall (surprisingly

now at eye level) asked: *where were you
all this time that you are finding me new?* Which is to say,
the delicate petals didn't ask but I do

wonder. How does one forget

    forget about running another marathon

    forget about kayaking through the Broken Islands

    forget about a trajectory more fortunate than this

> forget about carrying a mug of coffee, let alone
> my own weight
>
> forget about the calendar, appointments, erased.

Who says I must forget one thing to have another?
Who says happiness is a whole thing? I have my
functioning socket, my surgeon says
elements of what was can be again. *Not congruent
but something we can work with.*

Work with. With wonder.

Body Sensing Practice

1.
waking in a melt of stretcher sheets
and curiously some things have cleared

the hand on your chest
 are you coming 'round? how are you?
the voice tactile, arriving through fingers
into ribs and heart

bunched faces in a circle around you

all their easy questions like the bonus
questions at the end of an exam given
by the most kindly head examiner

a reward for being here
and you—so pleased to know
you got something right, finally

was it always going to be this easy?
as if all it took was for you to accept
the offers
  juice
  warm blanket

you enjoy every tube leading to your body
and its place here, the fluorescent glow
of the hallway, the falling footsteps out there
in the carrying-on world

each arriving as a gift
without ceremony
 you got this

2.
give me that leg
me flat on the physio bed
leg lifted not high not high at all
just let it go
let me hold it someone is saying
but how do you ever give over
the weight of bone and muscle
and flesh after all the years of carrying?
relax, let it go
and I release a few more pounds
to the hands down there
at the foot wonder if they are ready
who is ever ready for the dead weight?

3.
I don't want to go back
in there—he points—
the sharp titanium screw tip
protruding from the bottom
my rebuilt sacrum, the scan
all bone and metal,
not showing my butt
flesh, the soft flesh
Over time it will callus

      (so   sit)

Sit with this kernel,
my pose
 with broken sit bone

breathe: in deep
filling the absence
    out

cradle what has passed
and is now outside, beyond
    you

give it up

take in

release

2
WHEN THE TRIBUTARIES RAN RICH

Giving Back: the Dream

In the beginning, we stop.
Let out
our breath.
And turn
together, all
together in this
being.
It is easy
to dip into
purse and wallet,
give back the money.
Cede the land.
The bullets do not go easily
back into the barrel, the gunpowder
into the shell. To reverse
the reaction of charcoal and saltpeter,
sulfur and oxygen,
we called on our sciences.
Birds we reconstitute
as birds, people whole
people again.
Families of them.
We take back
the orders
of obedience,
un-till the land.
Younger and younger,
we shed our aged
layers. Fresh
as dream.
And when we wake
we begin
that dream-way.
Carry lightness.

My Place at the Corner

The wide-trunked trees of Chester Street are old
men, veterans in thick and cracked skin, aged-out soldiers
who look about to die yet stand on and on. Hold fast.

Broad arms raised in a great V—quietly celebrating survival,
the plain living: London planetrees bearing witness
to 80 years of street paving, pipe digging, and each year

a crew in orange vests, lifted in cherry-pickers, cutting
away, shaping a passageway for the powerlines
that loop to this pole at the corner. People here call them

Hydro poles, their stance in no way fluid, drawing their name
from the water of the North that drives its current across
British Columbia, over the strait, down-island to this country's tip.

There's an elegance in a power pole. I sketch
this one from across Chester, raise my pencil
to eye, testing its angle of repose. Absorbing

the skinned and planed trunk, cross-arm near the top,
looped wires, the grey barrel transformer. And more coils,
cable at the ready. Repair is assumed. It makes a good study

in pencil, then pen and ink. No flashy colours. So when I say
elegance I mean the elegance of simplicity. I try to keep it
that way, in my way, out of the way on a folding camp stool.

Nestled and observant and not a part
of the composition. The pole just there, leaning
with the confidence of a kid who has no intention

of going to school. Some days, a woman in a grey hoodie leans
against it, as if in mutual support, until the 17 University
comes along. Just here. The afterlife

of a Western red cedar as power pole
is 50 years, give or take. About half
as long as the London planetrees casting shade

from either side of the lines. In the wild,
Western red cedar can live 1000 years.
Is the wild a thing, anymore? I take the point

of my pen to the faint pencil lines, make them darker.
Harder. I'm going to wash this, later. Start
with phthalo blue, work in some grey.

You can't bury the lines, here on this rocky island. So the poles
stay, and the big arms of planetree reach around on either side
of the powerlines, as if crown-shy. Grey-brown.

I'll try some burnt sienna. No one cares
about the pole but every 40 years a new generation
of workers come to replace it. For now I will try

from my place at the corner to pay it due attention.

What Has Taken Place

city after city   street interventions
murals   front yard book exchanges   tactical
urbanism   last summer replanting Oceanspray   Stonecrop
in reclaimed parking stalls   hand-built seating slabs
    on Broad Street   island fir   painted in primaries

gatherings to talk   rethink   peel back
the layers   structure & idea / ideals   daylighting
    —midden—
buried creeks   sprung free from culverts   diverter pipes
   to splash   (hear that
   old dash—water over stone?)
      is it atonement
draws me to dig into remakes
at every landing place?
      is it some call back
to all those Daniel men who pulled up
and pushed on   the ones I can trace

generation after generation
300 years of plowing 'forward'
building over the old and storied
lands   claimed as new

—Jeremiah from South to North
Carolina   his son Basil
off to Arkansas   Levi leaving
for Illinois   Basil T chasing
California gold   my great grandfather
decamping for Washington State

Grandpa Charles snagging
homesteads on offer
to white settlers in Alberta—

and I who once thought myself a true
Alberta boy   settled/unsettled
in Coast Salish territory   at the land/water edge
      —driftwood—
on the shore's shifting line

what has taken place
here where roots of Garry oak
are paved over?   what stories
have been told of this
place?   what does placemaking mean
where place has been
taken?   taken over   meadow turned city
street   bearing the name of a Spanish
naval officer

who has taken this place?
not me I can say
in only the literal sense

placemaking is a verb   I hear
myself at every event I organize
in this capital   named for a 19th century head
of the house of Hanover

slowly I learn
to begin again
with invitation   bring offerings   unbox
cookies   open   eyes open   ears
today on the site
I kneel   creakily   kneepads borrowed
from our lead artist
      —new mural—
      —our thin new layer—
my brush following chalk   his lines

he brings his own
layered ancestry—
Michif / Salteaux / Cree / Scottish / English—
to these unceded territories

earns his place of respect

in this place we offer to help   return Lək̓ʷəŋən stories
to the public realm—a Songhees mural
over the blacktop   better
in that diminished way   this is
what we work with

drawing from a design
by a Lək̓ʷəŋən artist   her family
story   wolf ~ salmon ~ camas ~ orca
bright with the pulse of generations   rooted
like the Garry oaks that run under this
road up either side   and under it all
tar   asphalt   paint

cans at my foot   pried open
don't kick something over   I think   *try not to screw up*
shut my mouth when I hear that voice
yapping   pass the cookies

most days   they are eaten
become story

My Time Little

Hold on. Small hands flanked by grand paws
on the outer reaches. *Hold it true.* The iron wheel
nudging clockwise and counter, slow
as summer. Steady. True to the track, rolling
easy in cupped turf. One tractor tread to one rut.

The simple idea, gruffly taught. *Keep one true.*
The others fall in. Up and 'round hillock,
yesterday's work drawing a line today to follow.
Sputtering out to find cattle might have been
the mission. Work and desire lines in loose parallel.

Boy and old man, small, nestled into larger
history. The elder engaged in daily argument
with older land—give and take, cuss and coo.
That's the way. The way we make memory:
gather, track, herd.

Turning to home, clanking cows take their own line,
bump and bellow. Fall in. In their own time.
So long we animals linger on the way
that even this day, years long gone, a deep tracing
marks and holds. Patterns of intent and implement,

the rolling forth and back through generations.
Rolling grasslands long before we buried the elders, unearthed
the fine-grained gravel, long after the glaciers shed
their sediment. Before the cemetery stops and memory
stalls. And now on one day in 2020 much like all the others,

I walk a country road much like all the others, look up
every drive, through the familiar fan of field grasses,
along every furrow through soil. My eyes prize
each paired imprint of service and ceremony, wonder
how this trail or that might go, me now old, my time little.

When the Tributaries Ran Rich

We walk the waterfront, unleash
the dogs, toss sticks, gaze

to mountains resting on light
beds of fog. We are unfamiliar

with one another but for our
familiar clusters: woman with elderly
woman and walker; couples; tourists

with viewfinders, pointing. I too
point to the new-to-me: here, at the base

of Beacon Hill, in 1915, trenches
were dug thousands of miles from the front,

young men in training, digging
as deep as a rocky island would allow. Two years

I have lived here and the trenches are just another
invisible piece of my vast unknown. We miss so much.

*What do you miss most about growing up
on the homestead*, I asked

when my mother startled me saying she knew
about a better world I would never see.

Streams in the spring, she said, *so many.
Splashing through the day,*

even at night, a murmur. Her voice
just that. Then, stronger, *Now it's all culverts*

and cultivation and I swallowed. I wanted
to say I too had heard spring streams, sometime,

somewhere, but it was not the same.
She's been gone twenty years and still I feel

a rush to share something hopeful: *Did you hear,
the salmon spawning on the Columbia are almost back*

to the levels of your birth year, mom? But what's
this shortness of breath? She is gone.

In Grandfather Charles' time
the tributaries ran rich

with silver and pink, flashing and full,
flush with Chinook and Coho, Sockeye

Steelhead ten times beyond mother's
count. We cannot fathom. This November, hearing

of a good run of Chum up Goldstream we took
our boys down to witness: writhing

up the shallow, rubbing the rocks red
with death and the seed of tomorrow. Today

we are back on the seafront, where
dogs still chase sticks for no reason and each

of us gazes through mist toward what we hold
to be mountains, unmoored. As if

following some magnetic field, pulled
to a distant ache, origin unknown.

The Plow and What Follows

God speed the plow. . . . By this wonderful provision, which is only man's mastery over nature, the clouds are dispensing copious rains . . . [the plow] is the instrument which separates civilization from savagery; and converts a desert into a farm or garden. . . . To be more concise, *Rain follows the plow.*

—Charles Dana Wilber, 1881

Free Farms for the Million
Dominion of Canada
Climate the Healthiest in the World
Vast coal fields at convenient distances
Free farms of 160 acres
Open to every Male Adult of 18 years

—Recruitment advertisement,
Walla Walla Union-Bulletin, 1905

You might as well expect the rivers to run backward as that any man who was born a free man should be contented when penned up and denied liberty to go where he pleases. If you tie a horse to a stake, do you expect he will grow fat? If you pen an Indian up on a small spot of earth and compel him to stay there, he will not be contented, nor will he grow and prosper.

I have asked some of the great white chiefs where they get their authority to say to the Indian that he shall stay in one place, while he sees white men going where they please. They cannot tell me.

> —In-mut-tooyah-lat-lat (name translates from Sahaptin to English as "Thunder Traveling Over Mountains") known as Chief Joseph, was a leader of Wallowa band of Nez Perce, speaking in Washington D.C., 1879

Tack, Harness, Lash

Collars and bits and bridles and straps, blinkers
for some in the team. Great grandfather's fields,

their bodily folds of hillock and hollow, hold
thirty horses by our count. The cracked sepia photo.

Thirty horsepower pulling one threshing machine.
Our grandad Charles (so young) holds the reins,

rides a bench cantilevered high over the horses.
Three more men working the thresher: sack sower,

machine tender, header man. Bandanas around every neck.
The chute and steel gears and chain tilted towards us

on a rolling hillside of high grain outside Walla Walla.
My engineer brothers remark on the ingenuity. The horse smarts.

Lost to us. We laugh off our shared ignorance,
enjoy our ability to journey together with our deficits.

In the photos, the narrative we inherit, we see
no Walawalaláma—Walla Walla—people, walking the high plateaus,

paddling the grand rivers set in the land's rolling creases. We see no
measles, smallpox, no villages emptied of man, woman, child.

What an empire of privilege those Daniel men
were hitched to. Soon after harvest, at age 18,

Charlie would drive a one horse rig
North up the Spokane valley, through

the wide flat streets of the city of Spokane, its tens of thousands,
up to Kingsgate crossing, through the south east tip of British

Columbia to northern Alberta where quarters were free
to any man who proved up five acres

a year. A toehold for the right kind of settlers.
How was this possible? Charlie asked no questions,

I am sure, about how land came to be 'free,'
how some possibilities expand

while others shrink and die. This was the way.
The way a clan moves, carting claims.

State to state, territory to territory. Unsettling
to settle. So recently up from Oregon territory,

kept 'clear' by *Oregon Lash Law: Negroes*
"be they free or slave—[shall] be whipped

twice a year until he or she shall quit the territory."
Our ancestors buckled down, tack and harness, lash

and fence post, worked the homestead, worked
empire. Sod storehouses, sweat and fire, stumps pulled, stock

bred, fed and watered. Not nearly the first here.
The traders had been through with their iron pots.

Guns long and short, knives, blankets, disease.
Land agents with their own kind of branding,

selling The Inland Empire. On the assumption, always,
that empire, our empire at least, is a good. The way

we dream it. This photo is a still from the middle of a story.
Imagine going back, moving forward. To hold this image

is to hold a wealth, a debt. Possibilities, responsibilities. To hold
hardship, deficiency, loss. To hold them together, two reins

you have been handed.

Lang may yer lum reek

Donald MacLeod sailed back to Stornoway, strode
proudly back to kick about in the peat
among the blackhouses at Knock

on Lewis—born and raised—bragged

a wee bit about his herd. Not to be believed,
the old Gaels said, so many head in so few years.
Mind—Herefords, not highland longhairs.

Still, prize-winners, at his word. And voted
into parliament, he was, Donald over there
in his dominion. Canada. So many MacLeods

gone that way. Untethered from croft
if not clan. Aye, aye, make of it
what you will.

Ways to Find Family in a Forest

1. Uproot the Family Tree and Dig

There, in the fine filaments,
the dirt-clinging roots, you

might unearth a family
of one. Passing through Utah

stop, take in this stand
of aspen: its airy show—

sticky buds, fluttery leaves,
whispery bark, trunks in the thousands.

Standing, waving expressions
of the great heart of the single

being. Because below ground this
colony of male quaking aspen

thousands of years old is found
to be one entity, given one name: Pando.

What does it mean to count the rings
when each trunk is an offshoot

of the one rooted thing?
In the dirt the many are one.

2. Scrape Your Boots

Everywhere I tread I trail invaders,
aggressors. English ivy, Scottish
broom, giant hogweed. Volunteers. Constance
Hopkins, 14, stepped
off a cracked and creaking merchant ship,

November, 1620. *A Voyage to Plant the First
Colony in the Northern Parts of Virginia.*
Shivered, nearly starved, Constance—clueless
as her parents. As you or I in calling this
a new land. Nauset corn sustained
them that brutal first winter. A version
of the story has the Nauset giving corn. Another:
the Pilgrims dug up (stole) a Nauset cache. Each
has its believers. And perhaps, I think, there are two
truths, overlapping.

In spring, the Pilgrims rejoiced
at the first new growth: a five petal
flower they named Mayflower trailing arbutus. Itself
rare now, with habitat loss. Once it disappears it rarely
returns. Only 1100 people of Nauset descent carry on
their bloodline through the Mashpee Wampanoag.
I am one of 75,000 (give or take) descendants
of Constance, who bore 11 children, lived to 72.
We 75,000 track across this continent and beyond.

Accordion Map

Is there an instinct to draw
lines over land, to follow
what then unfolds? This map crosses
continent, territories and terrain—
inaccurate and in unexpected ways
terribly accurate. Annotated by hand,
its many bones now sleeping
in soil. The map fragile
as its paper turning
dust, outliving its maker, the idea
handed down.

Imagine a new panel open
as ocean, blank and featureless
the way we imagine bodies
of water, imagine my head buried
in the fold. I could be
the map
maker, the draft
animal, blinkered
in accordion folds, pleats
that breathe and wheeze
before their air leaves
as music.

3
IN THE FAMILY NAME

Kettling

Late summer heat and I look up
from the dock for the distant high

swirl of the big birds, their arc.
It's the season turkey vultures gather

here at island's edge for the lift
of rising thermals. A spiralling up,

ancient stirring. I mill among strangers
outside U.S. Customs, Victoria Harbour,

await the weary heave of the Coho ferry,
heavy with the years of crossings, coats

of marine paint. The old boat bumps up
to the dark fender, the deep piles. Oily hawsers

tossed to shore hands. We tuck away passports
and board. Every few years, my siblings and I

venture back to poke at ancestral places and deeds, soils
here and there, evidence of the built, broken, well

used and discarded. We will meet over footings
sunk beneath stratified lives as they decompose

or lay inert. Foundations. Will visit to toe
the edges, family seekers of hatching-places.

A stilled mill where a once-dammed stream
slides, spills fresh and cold over abandoned

brick, slabs of concrete polished smooth. Plunges
on cheerily. My sister, the youngest, will unroll

her multicoloured map, its tracing of tracks back.
From Canadian homesteads and oil rush, back. The Inland Empire.

California gold rush. Oregon Trail. Illinois Indian War. One generation,
two, five, ten. Pushing in the line that leads to us, pushing the deadly

edges of an empire of pride. Daniel name and exploits attached
to this Island, that Point, Place, Crescent. Which

Daniel was where, when? We list names, enlist imagined
lives. Restless. It's a big map, a continent of pink and blue and yellow

highlighter lines. A sheet of art
paper wide as my wingspan. I wrestle with the white

expanses of displaced and dead, this cleaned-up
track of a family's migrations, evasions, invasions.

We shall see what culture-clouded eyes allow. I look up
again for *Cathartes aura*, ancient birds, their heat-sensing eyes,

death-adapted. That great bulb of brain
adapted to catch the waft of decay a mile

overhead. Where are our vulture guides on this
edge of the continent? It is called kettling, the gathering

of vultures and this is the season of return, the time
for their sweep of community. What we call instinct

helps them find an updraft to carry them
over the Salish Sea to the peaks

south and winter range beyond. A float plane
screams through gull cries, deposits

a whiff of kerosene, lifts off. And our ship
groans, backs slowly away from the dock, rolls out

onto the swell of sea, toward
the toothed ranges of the ancestors.

Approaching Magnolia

> ... *experience doesn't just change what you see,*
> *it changes what you look for.*
>
> —Charan Ranganath, Why We Remember

Slide into a familiar rented Caravan and notice
the Daniel Island signs overhead, breeze
up Ashley River Road. Lazy acreages, tidy
white plank fences, white faces. Beyond
the African American Cemetery.

Approaching Magnolia with phone map
and unease. Fragments of information
stranded in the white matter, the folds
of my not knowing.

Billie Holiday arises somewhere back there
in the hidden neurons. Heavy, drifting, drugged lament.
    Scent of magnolias, sweet and fresh,
    Then the sudden smell of burning flesh.

Beyond the mouth of the Ashley, bypassing
Charleston slave mart, pushing up the throat
to the choke point. Magnolia. Offloading the chained
Gullah women, men, children from the heaving, putrid
ships of Portugal, Holland, England, Spain. Magnolia.

I read so much that I don't
absorb, retain, use.

Magnolia. Just a word, a place association
that I want to connect. Magnolia, Alberta, mid-way
between the MacLeod place
on Lake Isle, the Daniel place at Entwistle: did my parents
meet at that different Magnolia? Theirs and therefore mine
were and are not this.

White greeters wave happily and motion: park here for Magnolia.

Improbable magnolia blooms. Bright candelabras
of creamy petals bursting free
before the first spring leaf. Soft, silky,
tough. Millions of years
before the buzzy lightness of bees, petals strong
enough to support a beetle for pollination. Magnolia.
> *Because the family is quite old and has survived many*
> *geological events (such as ice ages, mountain formation,*
> *and continental drift), its distribution has become scattered.*

Read and hold this Magnolia Plantation and Gardens spread in
Charleston Life
> *Plan Your Visit with Travel & Leisure! A Day Trip:*
> *Nature Tour, Plantation House, Audubon Swamp,*
> *Zoo or the Romantic Garden.*
> *Special events: Ladybug Day. Fright Night.*
> *Share your vows in a memorable Magnolia wedding.*

Magnolia.

Choose to stay overnight in a cold cabin with Joseph McGill Jr.
and the Slave Dwelling Project. Or don't
choose. Yet stay, be held through malarial summers
for a generation, two, three, four. At Magnolia, 174 years
of choosing profit, choosing
misery.

Dripping Spanish moss, camellia
rich on the nose, swamp-sticky on skin. Gators.
A sign. *Watch your step.*
> *—Magnolia management*

Visit the Romantic Garden.
> *I like to say the definition of a romantic garden*
> *is an 'Extravagant Liar.' Truly, this is what a romantic*
> *garden is designed to do, to "lie" you into forgetting*
> *the normality of everyday life. Romantic Gardens are designed*

to take the viewer to a place where emotion takes precedence over reason.

On this normal day I revisit
the Magnolia lie, visit a place where child was
torn from mother, husband from wife, to make this
place easy. The easy life for a property owner,
enslaver, who looked a lot like me. Magnolia.

Choose your approach carefully. Magnolia.
    Approach me as you would a crime scene.

In the Family Name

You can't abandon your history and it won't abandon you.

—Jake Adam York

1.
Lift the lid of my laptop and out spills
the document in the hand of Joseph Daniel,
7X 'great' grandfather, deceased 1800,
Edgecombe, North Carolina.
Last will and testament of a patriarch,
assigning, distributing.
Abandoning.

> *to wife Sarah, 2 negroes, household and kitchen furniture*
> *to son Nathan Daniel—negro Dick*
> *to sons Josiah and Asa—negroes Dinah and Abram*
> *to daughter Zilpha Dickenson—negro Nancy*
> *to son Stephen—negro Rose*
> *to son Levi—negro Tom*
> *to daughter Delanah Barnes—negro Jack*
> *to daughter Martha Daudna—negro Jury*
> *to daughter Sally Daniel—negro Sip*
> *to my son Ephraim—all my remaining lands and negro*
>   *Lycey*

There. That. Names taken and given
by one Joseph Daniel.
Can I own this, release
his sense of ownership?

Dick, Dinah, Abram, Nancy, Rose, Tom, Jack, Jury, Sip, Lycey. Two
unnamed. How many families? Pulled apart
at the death of Joseph, assigned
here, assigned there. Land ownership,
property ownership, makes it easier
to find people, our people. Yet
not the Gullah people. No Gullah family links

in this record. Journeys not highlighted
in bright blue and pink and yellow
on our genealogy map. Oh the absences
in my trackable family.

Stories, grief, celebration. Distance, absence, loss. Where to start,
as a Daniel bearing the name of an English
enslaver, where to even begin? Broken people
along broken lines, generation after generation,
documented as furniture, if at all.
And, here we come—seven generations removed, a country
removed, 3000 miles removed—gone away and back
with our riches and free travel, returning to the ties, to touch
what binds, to wonder what releases
the knotted, twisted, tangled. What hangs,
       even now,
from strands thinned and frayed.

Dick, Dinah, Abram were the names
they were 'given.' Or, rather, not given
but punished with, sounds
foreign to the Gullah ear.
Nancy, Rose, Tom, Jack, Jury, Sip and Lycey.
I say the names, hear
the difference in the way I carry
my own name on my tongue.

2.
Genealogy drew us here, inheritance
twisted through centuries. Siblings
and spouses, ten of us, fortunate
to get along still, our family
tics and biases baked-in. Fortunate
to carry passports and credit cards that carry us
where curiosity leads. And here in South Carolina a descendant
of enslaved people talks
of how his people,
Gullah people, were herded
off foul galleys, paraded

onto platforms, bartered over. Back-breaking
cotton-picking, blood-sucking disease-carrying
mosquitos, lashings, hunger, fear, the danger of the wrong
eye contact. He looks us in the eye
and my eyes stray to a branch
just over his shoulder. Do we have questions?
Too many, and. And not enough.
    Listen.
    Ignorant.
    We process.

Rich Magnolia, florid Azaleas drooping history.
Air too humid, too heavy, too much
for we cool Canadians. Invasive vines
climb the grand old trunks, twist
and rope around oak and palmetto. Hanging, draped.

This is where our people came from.
Where they were comfortable.

Fugue and Spiritual

South Carolina, 2015

Step into the Magnolia manor, past
the white colonnades, White staff, as if
into a museum to kindness, into calm
and finery. Bone china, the lashed backs
of heirloom hickory
chairs *please do not sit*   the deep dark
oval walnut dinner table.
Is a fugue being played
in the parlour—the light
counterpoints, the mathematical
sequences? This third Big House
owned even now by the Drayton family,
fifteen generations in. Polished as a southern matriarch,
foyer armoire and rippled looking glass
reflecting faces as if through the ages. A narrow view
down this long white
corridor of power where we pause
before stern and starched portraits,
                                       enslavers
                                       stiff and righteous
and hauntingly familiar. As if family.
Politely Canadian, I have no other template,
ask a weather question
of the only Black staffer
imagine it's pretty hot here in the summer?
and he calmly, patiently, explains
how the faces on display here
fled the heat, the malaria, fled North
to summer homes while just over there,
on the bank of the Ashley, the enslaved
heaved bales onto rafts, destined
for the downriver markets of Charleston Cotton Company.

Imagine the haul, the drift of White wealth
by river and trail and rail, through the generations

to me. Drift is too loose a word. Let's call it
open shift, straight up compensation. Amidst the story
of the ancestors' migrations I hear
the call and response of the spiritual
the flight and act of fleeing

> *steal away, steal away home*
> *I ain't got long to stay here*

river so slow, out the front veranda, down the dappled lanes
—all shade maple and oak, weeping willow—and my lord
the intoxicants. Carolina Jasmine in the air. We walk the lane
that leads past alligators and marsh
alongside four siblings, emerge
at a row of plain one-room slave cabins,
meet our Black teacher. He lines
us up
        —please sit—
on a bare plank bench, sizes up
the five of us, facing him.
What does he see? A family
or more lived in each of those rooms,
he starts in, generation after generation, and
                —good question—
who counted as family
if your family was chattel
goods, items on a list
with pots and pans? Implements.
In a White man's will, White man's hand,
                who counted?
Did you count as family the broken
relations, the ones sold
down the river, passed
down to the kids, grandkids
even?
    How did the ancestors, my
    kin, enslave?—I mean,
    to enslave is to work hard
    at breaking what is human

between us, the cord, family
links—mother to son, father
to little girl, in favour of iron
implements, paper money.

To furrow soil and skin and feed
something we call the economy

        —enslave—
        —entrench—
        —enforce—

The sorrow lays heavy here
in wills and deeds, in the bloodline. Embodied.
Layered, fertile, recomposed. Humus we toe.

Then we get up and go. Not hurriedly, yet
we go.

Of another time, Magnolia, Big House, fugue,
slave cabin, spiritual. Vestiges, echoes, and reenactments,
too: here, in our time. The tempo and tone
playing out now.

4
EPISODIC TREMOR & SLIP

Night, Vectors

parents brought up from the deep well
of dream   float   buoyed   mute
weight slips rope over pulley   lifts them to silent wakefulness
     was it sound?   tremor?
unmeasured   untimed   something planetary
realigns as they roll and wait
house rounding into soft focus   caught
in satellite's play   bathed in the bounce of moonlight

then,
    sound sprung
one   *boing*
    metallic   spacey
so distant from the beat and breath of their bodies

gaping time and then   again
                boing
hearts jump
they push back the curtains of sleep
did you hear that? is that him out there?
    yes him   kicking up
from the family trampoline   drifting back   parabolic

slow motion   tumbling   they stumble into slippers   shudder down
stairs in unbuttoned nightshirts and flap out into the yard   calling
him   half grown boy bouncing   still in pjs   face a blank
bright planet   nightwashed   asleep
                in timeless orbit
again they call   coax
wake up please
and his body grows weighted
with awareness   more earthbound
each tumble and turn until coltish he wobbles
to the padded edge
where after long minutes
he blinks and croaks
and when the three of them cross

the yard to the house slip cautiously through wet fresh lawn
they do so hand-in-hand   tethered
if only in flesh

Fluency (First Loss)

At age three he wakes talking,
slowly pulling fog and frogs from *froat*,
re-finds his eloquent dream and arrives
at his sister's door fluent.
J questions and quarrels, explains
and defines, tries new words
and ties sounds 'round his tongue.

Strangers blink at his buoyant greetings
and his mom wonders what might be
too much. Our youngest tells his life story from this moment
backwards to anyone who listens and also
to those who don't.

He chatters in his safety seat on the way home,
chews his way through words with supper,
and sentences trail behind him out the door
into the cool evening yard.
The phone rings, Dad calling
from another time zone,
and J comes running to
the huge apparatus his mom holds down to his ear,

then falls silent. His eyes
roll, searching for sounds
tumbling out of nowhere into his head and he stands
in quiet wonder.

The moment passes, he dashes
to his room to play, leaving
mom to explain
this is not typical
he's always talking
I can't shut him up

As she put the phone down she hears him,
up in his room, talking, talking,
opens his door to find him
cross-legged on the floor,
the Fisher-Price phone in his lap.

I talk to my Daddy he explains
and turns back to his plastic phone with news
of backyard battles, trains, the string of syllables
making some perfect sense.

Well into the night, he swings
from story into song. The halting rhythms
hypnotic as his voice rises and rises
until with one high note he slips away.

Play Bonded

At 4, buckled in his safety seat, anchored
in motion, he belted Springsteen full throated
>   *Bonded in the U-S-A!*
>   *What means bonded?*
"Born. Born in the U.S.A." I meet his bright blues
in the rear view. "Babies are born, animals are born."
>   *Bonded again please?*

Strapped under basscans at 14, blinkered
under hoodie, leaning into heavy beats
as if harnessed to ancient barrow, self-dubbed
DJ Crush nods to mufflewhomp,
lids flat. Here not here.

Episodic Tremor and Slip

We learn geology the morning after the earthquake.

—Ralph Waldo Emerson

Episodic Tremor and Slip (ETS) is a process that occurs deep below the Earth's surface along faults that form the boundaries of tectonic plates. It involves repeated episodes of slow fault slip of a few centimetres over a period of several weeks, accompanied by seismic tremors.

—Natural Resources Canada

1. We Step In

There is no place to start with the mess.
Clothes crumpled, sills stained, grime
on every surface, flat
and vertical. Stench. Blinds down. A cat.
There sits our son, sullen and hunched, head
clamped under headphones. We can no longer start
from hope, we can only approach, sit
in our responsibility and listen when he rants
about landlords, employers, multi-fucking-national
corporations. The great forces
that push him around.

He is 27 and will go nowhere with us, will not travel
this territory, will not reason and accommodate. The place shakes
with his explosions, his booming. Plates rattle, cleavers tremble
and hearts jumping we are in full retreat again.

We live in retreat, making plans
for the wrong emergency. Prepare
for what has passed. There is always hope,

friends say. Friends didn't see that basement
suite we rented for him the fall we hoped
he could go back, finish a high school course.
The landlord calls. We step in
and here's a window screen, flimsy
frame wobbling, mesh cut out. Knife blades
scorched into enamel, the kitchen range stripped
down to bare burners. Someone needed to get closer to the flame.

Soon he will sell his dead car for less than he owes, fly
to the East Coast where he knows
no one, and over time we will
locate him, go, sit again. Listen.

I don't want to go on.

2. In the Absence of Answers

When did it start?
Age 12, even 10, when the teacher described his
drive-by friendships? Those meds we allowed him
to take for acne, was that the start, a bad complexion?
The fine print of contraindications, for Christ's sake?

Down at the bistro, he chops cilantro, shaves ginger, heats
up *a mean reduction*. Skin in the game, angry red
stove burns up one arm, down the other. Skincrawlers
across his forehead, speed bumps picked
open, unhealed. Healing he can't allow.
He sweats through erratic hours and asks for more,
cash pay. *No fucking way they're taxing me
to build destroyers down in that shipyard.*
Cash to buy kitty litter and kibble
for the Himalayan he feeds before himself.

We get him to sign a consent with the latest doctors
so they can talk to us. In the absence of answers,
we share a few familiar phrases, roll them back
and forth between us, as if rolling a combination lock
that might tumble open, release the happy child.
And, no, that's not going to happen.

3. Small Matters

Another job lost five weeks ago, *no biggie*,
he says, didn't want to upset us, scraping up
rough unready words now
through the smoked-out booze-burnt throat
and—wait for it—there's the matter
of rent. When I phone his grandmother
I mention neither. Such are the ways
we believe we lift ourselves above the common
mantle of our lives. Little tricks.

Remember, as a kid, on a perfect summer day,
when a push suddenly sent you skidding
down a slope, how gravel embeds
in the darkened skin of your knees? Earth's
grit in your blood. And you jump
back up, bite your tongue ever so gently? Substitute
the small hurt for the other one.

4. The Troubled Children

Daybreak early, nightmare late, the Troubled Children return,
bump up the side step, stumble us all awake.
The Troubled Children do not ebb and flow
like the others, through college and career fairs
and girlfriends, boyfriends. They reverberate through
the night, announce themselves with bells and pounding,
back where it all began. The unsurprising
upheaval. Duffle bags, heavy with ragged
remains, their broken and useless armour, dropped
on the landing. Rumble and rubble. Again. So little to show
for the emergency cash, the good talk, that last
fresh start.

So you, Parent of a Troubled Child, peer
through the blinds. At 5 a.m. you open the door
because there is no value in more damage. Bend
to lift what is piled at your feet. By 6 a.m., first pot
of coffee drained, you and all your invisible members
of the League of Parents of Troubled Children have resigned
yourselves to the old stories. Composed, edited
so the pieces almost adhere, ready
for the world of the not troubled.

May we, The Parents, trouble you with this?
The Troubled Children are not children.
And we are all children.
We are all troubled. We teach
unbelievable things all the time
like last night's community workshop about
continental drift, two and one half centimetres a year
right under us. So tiny. Imperceptible. Forgive
those who can't believe in tectonic plates, or those
who believe and can't bear to think, every day,
of all the fault lines. We The Parents keep
an emergency kit in the hall closet. Fake readiness.

5. Always the Fly

Important shit, this—eviction,
creditors, heat, water, food
money and always in the soup with us

here, not here, touch and go, buzzing up
an ear, brushed blind-handed, stupidly
back, always, one common housefly. Since

the Cenozoic. Adapted to flat booze, fresh
gut-throw, adapted to climbing walls,
to rocketing straight at ceilings, flip and stick.

Domestic as doors mis-hung to hang ajar,
windows missing mesh, droning one note always—
the song of yesterday, today, tomorrow, the layered

decay of days.

6. Plan B

We always had a Plan B except Plan B never worked
any more than Plan A and all subsequent plans
became named Plan B, over and over, so really
we should have been numbering them B1, B2, B3.
Where would we be now? B52? The bomber or the retro
rockers? Shrug. *Whatever.* Football. Hockey. Piano.
Judo. Katimavik. We always knew what needed to happen
(training? rehab?). But here we are. Not knowing. Reduced.

7. Calls from Across the Continent

I'm on a bike ride, or in a distant airport, or at a dinner, or
the wedding of a niece. His number comes up.
     Hello   ugggh   I'm dying
I tilt the phone away from my ear
when the dry heaves begin, having learned.
He can't keep water down. Doesn't want a cab
or ambulance to take him to care.
     They don't do anything for me   blaaaagh   dying

When did you start drinking?
This time, I mean. How many
hours, litres? How recently
did you stop? Did you stop? Look,
what can I do?
     You can't do anything

Every few hours, his thumb pushes
our speed dial as if to deliver a fix.
Water, I say. Hospital, I offer. Detox. Water.
My words an intravenous drip of sorts.
     blaaa—ugh

I sleep. At 3 a.m. another call and he
is ready, he says.
     Call an ambulance. Call.

8. Night Rescue

I wake and she's calling out
again, that struggling, heavy voice, distant
and right here beside me, gasping, the impossible
urgency of deep dream. Desperate, disoriented.
I rock and steady her, murmur *honey, honey*,
pull her alongside my body. Hold on.
This part of the night rescue is easy, familiar.
Then, awake, we just float, eyes
open in the dark.

9. Bringing It Up

Sure, we can talk about the drinking.
So much harder to talk about the thirst.
> *Don't you see the connections? Why do you think*
> *I'm vegan? Because they cut the beaks off*
> *birds and stick them in cages and sell us all*
> *Chicken Finger Specials. Don't you see?*

One day, the grief came shuddering up
and broke from below his ribs. He threw
a fist through the plaster. Quaking. The sobs, the great
gasps, rolling up and out.

Lately, all that comes out is puke and blood.

10. Blacklist

Leaving a Halifax hovel where mattresses
slump against a side fence, chain link
cut open, next to a dry pool tank, its empty
cans, fast food wrappers, faded. Flags
in the windows, hip-hop booming, voices screaming
fuck this and fuck that. Locks that don't.
We are filling a dumpster again. Stained,
broken things. Abandoned. Moving him
out of a bachelor suite he shares with a beautiful brown
American Pit Bull Terrier that "buddy" abandoned
here and we don't ask who buddy is. Buddy is
always the same guy, only different. Silky soft
and shy, the dog can't stay, can't go with us.
We coax her into the no-pets rental car. She sighs,
lays her heavy head in my wife's lap and snoozes.
At the animal shelter, she is
refused. A blacklisted breed. Here and all
neighbouring jurisdictions.
                                        What?
What do you do with a creature
no one wants, with a soft
inadmissible soul? We plead,
threaten to unleash her in an alley, plead some
more, offer a healthy cash donation. The dog
is too good for all this. We have known
her for three days and can somehow
imagine sleeping in a deserted alcove
with this dog, just sharing her warmth.
When the shelter consents, finally, my hand goes limp,
the leash falls free, a tremor passes
without notice of the world.

11. On Alert

He agrees to fly west, perch near us,
here on the Juan de Fuca fault. *Makes
no difference to me.* Does detox. Gets clean.
Goes to work, hauling his battered case
of knives from one kitchen to another. High-end, then
the pubs and family grills, then whoever will take him.
Another eviction, furniture abandoned
on the lawn of a kind and weary landlady. We take in
his cat. Clean her up, a cute lion
cut. The cat unimpressed.
One morning she stands alert, ignoring
us and her food. Staring, staring at
nothing, unmoving. Must be sick. Later
in the day, news of a 4.7 quake we never felt,
80 kilometres offshore. Right at the time
we put her food down. Oh, what we miss.

12. No Answer

We return the cat, return with armloads
of kitty supplies. Phone, text, lean on the apartment buzzer,
no answer. As we turn away, his roommate appears
at the door. *Uh, sorry I couldn't come right away,
I was just cleaning my handgun.*

13. Tracking

Parcels come back unclaimed, no texts,
no email answers, no voicemail, not-in-service
messages are the only messages. For two years.
Then, I see a hooded figure round the corner
from Cook onto Fort Street in a high-vis safety vest
bearing a cross and I'm on it
like a cop, calculating where he's going to be
by the time I get down that way. In the odd shadows
of night-lit shop windows it could be any one
of the Troubled Children. But—there—another angle,
as the signal switches amber to red. Slouching
west where the one-way runs east. Jesus,
he's gotten big. Bearded, heavy, drooped,
shuffling. His broad back
a continent, moving slowly away.
I drive to the end of the block, park,
get out, look both ways. I find
myself thinking
something about hope. I walk up the dark street
he is coming down.

5
UNTIL THE SEAS GRACE YOU

In the Family Support Circle

She had me
fooled. Thought
she had a flu when
it was withdrawals.

It felt like a rollercoaster ride,
a rollercoaster wearing blinders. We didn't know
where he was, where we were
going. I felt like throwing up.

I can think of nothing
and everything shifting
in my folding chair, eyes
on the floor and where do I start

>it's almost funny now
>those nights when we lived
>on the 21st floor with the baby
>just a wee bundle, me working
>my first "permanent" job
>at Emergency Preparedness
>and Saturday nights or more like
>Sunday morning at 2 some drunken joker
>would pull the fire alarm so we could
>just for fun walk the 21 floors, 42
>flights to stand with chattering teeth
>in the flashing red and what really
>has that got to do with these people
>here to escape the havoc and did I even
>speak?

that's all I got
I got nothing

Eyes on the floor, quiet
and growing, the hollow
absence at the centre of our circle.

Until the Seas Grace You

When the call comes it's always hundred-foot waves,
search and rescue, transport and triage. Jump in,
keep heads above water until the seas grace you
with a few seconds between slams.

Halifax or Victoria, Atlantic coast or Pacific
the same. The call comes after months of not. Grab
your flotation devices and wade into wreckage.
This is no time for salvage. No point reaching

for that falling photo of the last family
Christmas gathering, the crusted laptop
once gifted. Simply stay out of the crashing debris.
By now, you know the rescue routine. No longer parents:

first responders, divers, geared up 24/7
ensuring the basics. Oxygen. Evacuation.
Then the dangerous calm, when you think
you can take a breather, before the echo
waves hit. Big swells of unpaid bills, stray

animals, abandoned roommates with needs.
Fatigue, resentment, recovery repeated
on an asymmetric cycle, as tides
respond to the pull of moons, festive

dates circled on the calendar. Patterns
of trauma, predictable and not, like a life. Over
these wrecks, don't linger. Don't
return expecting sunken treasures.

Alarm Will Sound

Mental Health is a tower hundreds of stories high
in thin air. The descent trashes you. Weighted
boots, unworldly gravity on grated steel rungs
ringing step by step down, landing to landing,
floor by floor.

High above, distant, delayed, the small click
of the door you came through.

The only way out now through a fire
door at the bottom, heaving against the bar.
For Emergency Use Only.
On the other side a wail
bulleting around a concrete bunker.
Disoriented, finding yourself now
below ground level—twelve steps up.
If you can, if you can.

Conscripts

We gather, participants and helpers, often
unclear who needs help, knowing
how every heart beats
with need. We gather
the way maple leaves stick
at the edge of the iron grate over the rainwater drain,
wet, together on a journey down from the high
branches, blown to the curb, swept
and left. *In honour of all those who have been
conscripted into the brotherhood of loss,* we cluster
a few times a week, walk downtown streets, jog
around the harbour on the better days, return to form
a wonky circle and stretch, share
a table of donated food. We earn
caps that sport our mantra: *Every Step Counts.*
A brotherhood, a sisterhood of quiet
talk about unimportant things. Our rule:
no personal problems, no prodding.
Simply attend. Simply attend.
Tuesday and Thursdays.
Beverly has left her home twice
this week. For this, only. Kyle takes his veggie wrap
with an eye on a possible second. Eleni mutters
Hellenic phrases under her breath,
practicing acrophonic numbers
to what end we never know.
Most often, we walk wordless
steps that serve as speech of sorts, each footfall
a testimony to movement. Respite in the moment
it takes to stride. A world made, quietly, tolerable.
We stick to this habit and are not yet swept to sea.

Search

Memory is movement, synapses beaming here
and there, ephemeral. Judges prefer to unlock

a solid chest of mementos. The expert witness says
there is no catching neurons. Only watching

their jump, here to there. Positive to negative.
Episodic flickers. Unsearchable. His scenes

leave us gaping: me, his mom, his siblings,
the hockey teammates he swears were right there

in the locker room. Real. Now, how to search,
recover? My old journals might hold a line

or two of insight but in that era days disappeared
onto disks. Unreadable now. Going back,

I gathered the old floppies from my gone
Kaypro, bought back archaic drives, recruited

techies to aid in the operation, but found
nothing backwards compatible. Bits of code here

and there but every version corrupted. Bytes fallen
victim: bad exits, malware, power issues.

Chasm and Divide

For a long time I held back
on recording, on wringing out, throwing
up my own stink. Always there were more tricks
to try. Sober days, moments
of fresh hope. Then one day I sighed
and simply said to him what I was thinking
not what he needed.

This is getting old.

Not what he needed.

*This is getting old and here is a bag
with a bunch of fluids to flush what ails
you and the truth beneath that is that I am
getting old.*

We are entangled and every knot and loop
of shared failure seems to tighten
until something falls away as we walk away
each in our own confused direction.

Maybe what he needed.

And now? Time's unspooling, the blur
of distance, helps. But there are no final words
to share. *This is getting old* is not the final
emptiness, anymore than getting old
is the final injustice, just another one.

Years, years, years. Sing the old song
that fades into a distant hum
barely audible
in the inner ear.

      \ \   / /

The divide is simple.

It is a divide not on a height but in a valley. Mariana Trench. Cold,
dark, dense with the weight of its depth.

The forms that live there were long thought
to be tiny, microbial. Unrecognizable
to us. Of late, trying to understand, researchers reveal
the opposite of the expected: deep-sea gigantism.

The Pacific plate is subducted beneath the Mariana plate.
The push toward mountains is the push toward valleys.

Is this perhaps tactical on behalf of the plates?
Even unseen, shifting away.

Our Kit

We're missing something. Gaps in our kit.
We understand the game. A moon mission

team exercise: what you need, don't need
for the unfamiliar, the hostile environment.

A team member stranded in space.
Plans best done by a group.

>   Fifteen items to rank: signal flares (dumb),
>   life raft (dumber?), tanks
>   of oxygen (that I get)
>   but everything in this game
>   can be second-guessed. Two pistols
>   with no mention of ammunition.

Alone, I miss some crucial element:
the fire starter, the warm wrap, batteries.

The two of us not much better: vacant
looks, one to the other, to our kit and back.

And the problem? Are we preparing for the right
rescue? What planet are we on? What moon awaits?

You Don't Get Here Without

Not a new thing,   estrangement, I like
how dictionaries emphasize
formerly close and   *affectionate relationship.*

In use since 1539.
Without   love, affection,
without
                                    years on the playgrounds
                                    hockey rinks, stickhandling, wordplay
there is no estrangement.

You don't get here   without being there.

It comes to this   after years of shifting
to and fro,
heavy bodies   casting silent shadows,
                                    moving
some sort of inarticulate absence
of conversation,   leaving

what radio people call dead air.

People don't send cards   mourning the anniversary
                                    of an estrangement.
We don't bury these
                                    lost days, years.

It takes at least two to be estranged. Yet at times
                                        it is as if
we are without human agency,
                                    stone dumb, slabs
on the thin crust of a tectonic plate,
                                    pulled slowly over molten core.

6
IN A SMALL CRAFT IN THE CURRENT

In a Small Craft in the Current

> It looked, didn't it,
> just like harmlessness.
>
> —Carl Phillips, *Speak Low*

It's too late
to learn to read
water, all my years
of failed swimming
lessons, tugging against
a current impossibly
deep. Fear slaps up
both sides of the kayak,
as if the sea or my seagoing
ancestors push to claim me, my bolted body
unbalanced in here, this vessel
narrow and its fibre
membrane so thin.

A breeze chops the flat
sea into little crests
I might have found attractive
from shore. I stab back at nothing
that will hold. Peter impressively still
in his lead craft at my prow, his paddle a horizontal
signal: pause here.
                    Here at the bottom
of James Island with a wide channel
daunting ahead, skies deeper grey
and the chop growing, a to-and-fro,
nervous energy.
    Five or ten, here.
His paddle now stirring,
as if a seaforce is but a stew
in a small bowl.
Why?

>   *We can fight it or we can wait*
>   *for a more friendly current. It will turn soon.*

How will we know?
>   *Kelp.* His paddle points
>   to the sway of bulbs below, leaning South
>   to open sea.

And when next we look, they bend
to point us North. Our intended direction.

Student ready, water teaches.

Emergency Triolets Breakdown

> Climate emergencies are a bit like buses. You wait an age for one and then three come along at once.
>
> —Adam Vaughan, *New Scientist*

1.
We drive because who's going to walk
through another storm worse than the last,
that storm of the century that gave us a little shock.
We drive because who's going to walk
all that way, think of the time, think of the clock.
The world is changing so fast
we drive because who's going to walk
through another storm worse than the last.

2.
They have such evocative names,
the developments that replace all the best places:
Spruce Meadows, Cypress Hills, Sweetgrass Plains.
So pleasing, so natural the new old names.
Suburbs and chemical plants take pains
to teach us about such evocative names
—do you remember all the best places?

3.
Sure we need to do something soon
about this whole climate mess, at least
there is talk we do. We sing the same tune.
Sure we need to do something soon
about all kinds of problems but, man,
politicians always mess it up.
Sure we need to do something. Soon.
But about this whole climate mess . . .

What Does Not Fall

Slow autumn, so heavy,
so uplifting. Garry oak leaves
crinkle and droop like tired tongues, drool

with chill morning dew and yet hold fast,
well beyond the trembling
aspens, my prairie childhood. Some shine
the way of well-used paper money, glint

of gold. Every day a few
tumble to the boulevards, accumulate.
This could go on

a month or more. No shivering bare
limbs. Yet. Is this what Keats loved?
Cling to this slowness. Wait. Join the watch

as Cascadia moves ever so grindingly.
Half an inch a year, plate over plate.
One day the earth will shudder.

Savour what does not fall.

Hush

Only what is unnamed is wild.

From a moss-covered cabin
down on the lagoon each day I walk, cross
the highway, up new streets christened
for what they destroy: Briarwood, Pond,
Hope. I have six days to retreat
from the emergencies, urgencies, plans
and pandemic. So I slip into Latoria Creek
ravine, a narrow notch, a dark
                    V
between housing tracts and gravel pit. Its path groomed
for city feet like mine. Blinkers of second-growth cedar
frame the banks, guard
the tailored fancy that we enter
some green
future, not
a moist and forgotten crease
in a fat man's belly. In the bush a murmur
escapes, a trickle, some
weak whisper.
                    Hush.
Before you name, just hush.

Lift

An ordinary thing is happening at the pink house

down the street, the storey-and-a-half clapboard
built a generation ago. Yesterday an excavator
(steel teeth and treads that shred the ground)
tore the footing out, stone and brick supports

made rubble. Today everything rests, shored up
on cribs. Swallows dip and dart through the curious
fresh shade, air suddenly open and available again, as
it would have been all those bird-generations ago.

This is common now in the neighbourhood,
remaking the old houses. New suites, new headroom
for all to grow tall and taller, my children's
generation, the next, and beyond. I see curtains

still on the windows, knick-knacks on sills. That gentle,
the lift. Next week the structure will be resettled
on a new seismic foundation and the subs
will run power and waterworks. Soon to the dismay

of swallows will come studs and siding again. Paint.
This stack of fresh two-by-tens will become new
risers and treads, make up the gap, step by step
from earth to entry. I who pause, then pass by

the little house only hope
it might remain pink
in its days beyond me.

wet/land/air

water plantain
swallow   cottonwood fluff
   sweetflag   bulrush
   dragonfly   mayfly
         mosquito

red-winged blackbird
        busy

     wet/land/air
         song

7
ELDERS AND THE LIGHT

Maple and Oak and the Light They Hold Aloft

We cannot hold up
forever. Cannot live up

to the brightness the elders hold
aloft. Those flickers in the high

canopy. What flutters
in the towering stands

beyond us now. We hear
the creaking. Fear the sway. Worry

growing heavy as lumber. The weight
of what might fall, the power of it all

coming down: trunks thrashing,
a roar through saplings, reducing

all to matchsticks, flecks, bits
of bark and dark green silence.

Witness in the Water

Here, desire and passage are written
in slant line that cleaves to the strata
of clay, a rut down the bank
where animals have followed

the sound and scent of autumn shallows.
Blue Rapids. I thirst too, pick across
river stones, wade out. High above, an osprey
circles, surveys. Plummets, strikes the stream

and spirals back up, quiet as
a stirring thought, drops—freefall—strikes—
and turns to climb, claws empty in the chill. Time and again.
Perhaps for the last time, I come here, aging, scratching

at the plain old mysteries, poking
sodded layers, seeking *a beautiful meadow
sufficiently large for a horse race*. Boggy Hall
trading post abandoned 200 years ago now.

Even the log cabin that dad helped grandpa build
eight decades gone. In my copy of an old photo
dad stands barefoot on the bareback of a horse
beside that cabin, in the meadow overgrown now

with poplar and pine. For ten years the grandparents
left a good farmstead on the rails for this. *Remote as hell*
a brother mutters, tips his eyes skyward. We will never know
why. They moved on. Logs gone to soil now.

Maybe a dozen times the bird falls and again
lifts from failure. Light slips. Shadows slide off the pines
and down the banks, deepen the water. I stand wet booted
on a gravel swale in the ancestral stream

while the raptor works on, silver in the slant
of light, disappearing into black pools. Each dive

brings the hunt further downstream until I look up
from a thought to emptiness. The river slips

around my ankles, passes,
braids again behind my heel
and smooths. Water, like time, leaving
its mark and keeping none.

A Run on Flowers

Spring bursts through everywhere,
pooling
so briefly. Air light
and lifting. A run on
flowers at the shop.
Nothing's up yet.
The selection thin,
a modest bunch
he grabs for her. When she asks
after their names he will not know.
Quilted to her bed, she should be up,
out walking, the south face
of each cracked and storied Grandview sidewalk
now free of snow. Melt
spilling off the lip of gutters, his car
idling in the drive.

She reached to catch a falling sister, them both
failing, the wheelchair rolling aside, she says. *Stupid.
I shouldn't have been so
stupid.* Her back out good
now. He waves the tinted pastel
petals and she raises a weak backhand,
gesturing to the bedside table. A magazine folded
open. *You should read about that author,
Margaret Laurence. She lived quite
the ordinary life.*

She smooths the quilt, her torso
and legs soft furrows. An eroding landscape.
It's a short season, she says. *That's all. Yes,*
he says. *Well,
I have to run.* Later, he will wonder
did he remember, even,
to put the flowers in water.

Absence, Not False

I return to the gap
the story mostly missing

       I'm unable to pull up a chair
       ask questions
       and that says
                        what
       about my caring

mother's missing teeth
                how
I never knew her
            before the false
teeth
      her cautious smile, hiding
her gums, appliances

ordinary terror

some stories bear never repeating

       those old brittle family photo albums
       where posed people fall out
       in your lap, unidentified

black pages blank now
but for the corner tabs

                ⌈   ⌉

                ⌊   ⌋

the way a chair
for most of its hours
will hold absence

The Thing

What happened is, it died in a flash
and sputter, the great mass of it
no defence to a spill of water. Snapping
back into the deep silence from which all things
sprang. We wiped it dry; when you polish
a dark thing, it gives back a version
of yourself.
                    Then we laughed,
"Oh well, it's just a thing," quoting mother
and her way with humour, its rich darkness.

Bouquets were everywhere that March day, every
time the bell rang, more. Family gathering, the living
room swelling with blossoms and teacups and cookies
on every side table. And what better place
to set a small globe, a bowl of blooms, but on the massive
Trinitron. Remember how the kids loved its
picture-in-picture? It was a monster, the apex
TV in the era before the flatscreens.

Three men had carried it in and it would take three again
to move it out. Some later day.
Enough of carrying, today. Today we remember
'it's just a thing,' mom's steady Scots take
on what we accumulate, what briefly
dazzles and possesses us.

Isn't it something, how loss gathers
us, puts a polish on hardness and humanity,
a shine dark and bright?

Our eyes, too, have a shine today
that we share, one to another. 'Just a thing,' we chuckle.

The thing is, she was so newly buried, mom,
and we needed to find ways to bring her back,
and so practiced laughing at the death of the thing.

when a loved one dies

when a loved one dies
and this will happen
when a loved one dies
(you know who
I mean) we will rise
to each task and push
documents back across the desk
make the calls that caller and called know
do not fit the pattern

we will rise as if ourselves
relieved of bodies
drift as if watching from on high

and at a time in the future
(there is a future) some say
weeks some say months or years
(you will not even notice the time)
your lungs empty and without thought
will open again as they do

but deeply

and their emptiness
the hole outside there in the world
is found inside you
becomes the invitation

an invisible something that inflates
you and feels like a lost life returning

To Carry an Absence

She smiled tight-lipped
over false teeth, her own pulled
too soon. Forever changed.

Our son's birthday is no longer circled
on the calendar, is an empty square, like
every other, a sequence of gone.

The miscarriages unspoken now, only
to rush back in the flush of dark
night, the wide awakening to nothing.

To carry an absence, that weighted
grief, practice an empty howl.
It carries. Gone, gone, gone.

To carry an absence, learn to lean
a little, not so anyone might notice, but just
to feel a certain balance shift.

Grave Work

Blocking our way in the middle of the walking path
through Pioneer Square, a long white Frontier,
tailgate down, stoneworking tools layered on the bed.

Two sturdy young men stretch a task, fill this hour like the last,
admire their measured pensionable progress, one face
of a black granite monument shining, three sides dull.

Surrounded by city, this small green was once
Victoria's only burial ground. Full by 1873, closed
and left to weed, wood rot, vandals and brambles.

In 1908 an administrator scraped the whole
clear, headstones pushed to the north edge, replanted
lawn grass, declared it a park. Everything, now, reversed

as if 100 years could be reversed, stones tipped back
up on new concrete pads, placed where someone today
thinks they once properly belonged.

Over in the east corner, more rejuvenation awaits
—crumbling headstones set off by fluorescent pink
plastic tape, loosely strung, stake to wooden stake.

Step around the idle
truck, in conversation
with muted stones, murmur
support for the work that never ends.

Biking to the Green Burial Grounds

Still breathing
heavily, borderline
giddy, we pull off
sweaty helmets. A stand-on-the-pedals climb
up cemetery hill caught us a bit
by surprise—burning
quads and emptied lungs—
unprepared, though we knew it was coming.

At woods' edge we stand
bikes, step into green
burial grove, rest
on a bench, contemplate the vigor
of bush and bees. This is the place,
the final place, where we will one day be
wrapped in plain cloth shrouds
and lowered. Simply planted. Become
the nourishment.

Odd, the vivid
energy today, flushing
through flesh that will slowly take its leave, abandon
our boneworks. Today our whole
being can sit a moment
in satisfaction, before we kick
our kickstands back. Today
we will savour the downhill
ride home, coasting
away.

Notes

The opening epigraph is from a conference presentation by Saidiya Hartman, "Archaeologies of Black Memory," University of Miami (2007), as quoted by Catherine Sasanov in *Slavery's Descendants*.

In *An Opening for the Uninvited*, the phrase 'a world that wishes you nothing' is paraphrased from the novel *Trask* by Don Berry. The poem's theme of welcoming the uninvited is inspired by Rumi's *The Guest House*.

What Has Taken Place is drawn from my work with Greater Victoria Placemaking Network. Hay'sxw'qa si'em to artists Jesse Campbell and Brianna Bear for their creative spirit and patient teaching.

Sources for the quotes in *The Plow and What Follows* are: (US) National Parks Service online article, 'James A. Garfield and "Rain Follows the Plow,"' https://www.nps.gov/articles/000/james-a-garfield-and-rain-follows-the-plow.htm; *The Evening Bulletin* Walla Walla Washington, 1906 (Library of Congress Archives); Edward S. Curtis and The North American Indian, Spring-Summer 2018: Chief Joseph of the Nez Percé, University of Pittsburgh Library System online.

The title of *Lang may yer lum reek* is Gaelic for 'long may your chimney smoke.'

The references in *Ways to Find Family in a Forest* are from the text of the Mayflower Compact and plant descriptions in GardeningKnowHow.com.

In *Approaching Magnolia*, the 'Approach me as you would a crime scene' quote is from Beverly Fulcher Bevel on the 'Linked Through Slavery' group website. The 'extravagant liar' definition of a romantic garden is a quote from Tom Johnson, former Executive Director of Magnolia Plantation and Gardens, on azaleas.org.

In *Fugue and Spiritual*, the reference to a 'museum of kindness' is in response to *Museum of Kindness* by Susan Elmslie.
The definition quoted at the start of *Episodic Tremor and Slip* is from the monograph "Episodic Tremor and Slip," Geological Survey of Canada (2011), Government of Canada, Sidney B.C.

Until the Seas Grace You is prompted by an online commentary on grief, of uncertain origin but attributed to "G. Snow."

The italicized line in *Conscripts* is from Edward Hirsch's "The Living Fire." Every Step Counts is the name of a walk / run program in Victoria, B.C., Canada for people with challenges related to addictions, mental health and poverty.

Chasm and Divide is modelled on Jeffrey Harrison's *Essay on a Recurring Theme*.

In a Small Craft in the Current is a response to the Carl Phillips poem *Speak Low* (Farrar, Straus and Giroux, 2010). Used with permission from the author. The concept of 'how to read water' is from Tristan Gooley's book of that title.

Emergency Triolets Breakdown is a sequence of three triolets that initially follow the traditional rhyme patterns of the form and then degenerate, come apart. The epigraph is quoted with permission of Adam Vaughan, from New Scientist "We're Living through a Climate Emergency. Time to Start Acting Like It," 20 June 2019.

In the poem *Witness in the Water*, the phrase *a beautiful meadow sufficiently large for a horse race* is quoted from the journals of Alexander Henry (1739-1834) about the Boggy Hall trading post in west-central Alberta.

The chair image in *Absence, Not False* was inspired by the Jane Hirshfield poem "A Chair in Snow."

Acknowledgements

With great love, respect and gratitude, this book is for Sandi Koop. Partners on the journey.

These are love poems. In them, I have done my best to honour the multiple lives and truths of friends, family and ancestors. My best is imperfect.

Thanks to my children, siblings and other family members for our shared journeys into family history (recent and distant), and for responding to the poems as they emerged. The family genealogical records are thanks to my sister Darolyn Daniel; any errors are mine. I appreciate the guidance of fellow members of Coming to the Table, a group that brings together descendants of enslaved people and their enslavers, for perspective on my South Carolina poems.

After being away from the literary life for many years, I returned with the sensibility of the novice, and immersed myself in writing programs through Pacific University (OR), Simon Fraser University (B.C.) and Bemidji State University (MN). My thanks to the writer / leaders in those programs, including Kwame Dawes, Jordan Abel, and Ada Limón, as well as fellow writers in the programs for feedback. Thanks as well to Sandra Ridley and Laurence Hutchman for reading and responding to the work. Special thanks to Bruce Hunter, Kelli Russell Agodon and Yvonne Blomer for substantive editorial feedback and publishing suggestions, and to Ellen Bass for much-needed encouragement.

Thanks to the editors of the following journals and anthologies for publishing earlier versions of these poems:

Empty Mirror
Red Wheelbarrow (U.S.)
Poetry in Your Pocket and *Poetry Pause* (League of Canadian Poets)
Prairie Fire
emerge (Simon Fraser University)
Juniper
FreeFall
The Senior Class: Poems on Aging (Lamar University Literary Press)

You are a Flower Growing Off the Side of a Cliff (chapbook, League of Canadian poets)
The Fiddlehead
Ex-Puritan

Finally, many thanks to the *Brave & Brilliant* team at University of Calgary Press for believing in and applying their talents to this book: Aritha van Herk, Brian Scrivener, Helen Hajnoczky, Alison Cobra, and Melina Cusano. Special thanks to Helen for deeply thoughtful and skillful edits.

Photo Credit: Taylor Roades

LORNE DANIEL is a Canadian poet and non-fiction writer. He has been deeply engaged in the literary community, including the emergence of a Canadian prairie poetry scene in the 1970s. He has written four books of poetry, edited anthologies and literary journals, and written freelance journalism. His work has been published in dozens of anthologies, journals, newspapers and magazines in Canada, the U.S. and the U.K. Lorne lives on the traditional territories of the Lək̓ʷəŋən people in Victoria, B.C.

 **BRAVE & BRILLIANT SERIES**

SERIES EDITOR: Aritha van Herk, Professor, English, University of Calgary
ISSN 2371-7238 (PRINT) ISSN 2371-7246 (ONLINE)

No. 1 ·	*The Book of Sensations*	Sheri-D Wilson
No. 2 ·	*Throwing the Diamond Hitch*	Emily Ursuliak
No. 3 ·	*Fail Safe*	Nikki Sheppy
No. 4 ·	*Quarry*	Tanis Franco
No. 5 ·	*Visible Cities*	Kathleen Wall and Veronica Geminder
No. 6 ·	*The Comedian*	Clem Martini
No. 7 ·	*The High Line Scavenger Hunt*	Lucas Crawford
No. 8 ·	*Exhibit*	Paul Zits
No. 9 ·	*Pugg's Portmanteau*	D. M. Bryan
No. 10 ·	*Dendrite Balconies*	Sean Braune
No. 11 ·	*The Red Chesterfield*	Wayne Arthurson
No. 12 ·	*Air Salt*	Ian Kinney
No. 13 ·	*Legislating Love*	Play by Natalie Meisner, with Director's Notes by Jason Mehmel, and Essays by Kevin Allen and Tereasa Maillie
No. 14 ·	*The Manhattan Project*	Ken Hunt
No. 15 ·	*Long Division*	Gil McElroy
No. 16 ·	*Disappearing in Reverse*	Allie McFarland
No. 17 ·	*Phillis*	Alison Clarke
No. 18 ·	*DR SAD*	David Bateman
No. 19 ·	*Unlocking*	Amy LeBlanc
No. 20 ·	*Spectral Living*	Andrea King
No. 21 ·	*Happy Sands*	Barb Howard
No. 22 ·	*In Singing, He Composed a Song*	Jeremy Stewart
No. 23 ·	*I Wish I Could be Peter Falk*	Paul Zits
No. 24 ·	*A Kid Called Chatter*	Chris Kelly
No. 25 ·	*the book of smaller*	rob mclennan
No. 26 ·	*An Orchid Astronomy*	Tasnuva Hayden
No. 27 ·	*Not the Apocalypse I Was Hoping For*	Leslie Greentree
No. 28 ·	*Refugia*	Patrick Horner
No. 29 ·	*Five Stalks of Grain*	Adrian Lysenko, Illustrated by Ivanka Theodosia Galadza
No. 30 ·	*body works*	dennis cooley
No. 31 ·	*East Grand Lake*	Tim Ryan
No. 32 ·	*Muster Points*	Lucas Crawford
No. 33 ·	*Flicker*	Lori Hahnel
No. 34 ·	*Flight Risk*	A Play by Meg Braem, with Essays by William John Pratt and by David B. Hogan and Philip D. St. John, and Director's Notes by Samantha MacDonald
No. 35 ·	*The Signs of No*	Judith Pond
No. 36 ·	*Limited Verse*	David Martin
No. 37 ·	*We Are Already Ghosts*	Kit Dobson
No. 38 ·	*Invisible Lives*	Cristalle Smith
No. 39 ·	*Recombinant Theory*	Joel Katelnikoff
No. 40 ·	*The Loom*	Andy Weaver
No. 41 ·	*Bonememory*	Anna Veprinska
No. 42 ·	*Love and War Western Style*	Rose Scollard
No. 43 ·	*Rag Pickers*	Blaine Newton
No. 44 ·	*What is Broken Binds Us*	Lorne Daniel